The Ballad of HMS Belfast

CIARAN CARSON was born in 1948. His other poetry collections include *The Irish for No* (1987); *The New Estate and Other Poems* (1988); *Belfast Confetti*, which won the 1989 *Irish Times*/Aer Lingus Irish Literature Prize; *First Language*, which won the 1993 T. S. Eliot Prize; *Opera Et Cetera* (1996), a Poetry Book Society Choice; *The Alexandrine Plan* (1998) and *The Twelfth of Never*. He has also published two books of prose – *Last Night's Fun* and *The Star Factory*. He lives in Belfast with his family.

CIARAN CARSON

The Ballad of
HMS Belfast

A Compendium of Belfast Poems

PICADOR
in association with The Gallery Press

First published 1999 by Picador
an imprint of Macmillan Publishers Ltd
25 Eccleston Place, London SW1W 9NF
Basingstoke and Oxford
Associated companies throughout the world
www.macmillan.co.uk

In association with The Gallery Press

ISBN 0 330 37369 2

1 3 5 7 9 8 6 4 2

A CIP catalogue record for this book is available from
the British Library.

Printed and bound in Great Britain by
Mackays of Chatham plc, Chatham, Kent

Contents

Pro tanto quid retribuamus

For so much, what shall we give in return.

Dunne

It was then I heard of the missing man.
The wireless spoke through a hiss of static —
Someone was being interviewed:
The missing man, the caller said, can be found
At Cullyhanna Parochial House.
That was all. Those were his very words.
I reached an avenue of darkened yews.
Somewhere footsteps on the gravel.

I then identified myself, and he
Embraced me, someone I had never seen
Before, but it was him all right, bearded
And dishevelled. There were tears in his eyes.
He knew nothing of the ransoms.
He did not know who they were. He knew nothing
Of his whereabouts. He did not even know
If he was in the South or North.

It seemed he was relieved from hiding in
Some outhouse filled with ploughs and harrows,
Rusted winnowings that jabbed and rasped
At him. He had felt like a beaten child.
When they hooded him with a balaclava,
He thought the woolly blackness was like being
Shut up under stairs, without a hint of hope,
Stitches dropped that no one could knit back.

From Camlough, Silverbridge and Crossmaglen
The military were closing in. He was,
It seemed, the paste on the wallpaper, or
The wall, spunked out between the leaves, etched
At last into the memories of what might have been.
He was released. The three bullets they had given him
As souvenirs chinked in his pocket. He slipped
Through a hole in the security net.

All day long for seven days, he had lain
On the broad of his back on the floor.
He could see nothing, but turned, again
And again, to an image of himself as a child
Hunched in bed, staring at the ceiling,
At the enigmatic pits and tics
That scored the blankness, and then, farther,
To the stars that brushed against that windowpane.

Dresden

Horse Boyle was called Horse Boyle because of his brother
  Mule;
Though why Mule was called Mule is anybody's guess. I
  stayed there once,
Or rather, I nearly stayed there once. But that's another story.
At any rate they lived in this decrepit caravan, not two miles
  out of Carrick,
Encroached upon by baroque pyramids of empty baked bean
  tins, rusts
And ochres, hints of autumn merging into twilight. Horse
  believed
They were as good as a watchdog, and to tell you the truth
You couldn't go near the place without something falling
  over:
A minor avalanche would ensue — more like a shop bell,
  really,

The old-fashioned ones on string, connected to the latch,
  I think,
And as you entered in, the bell would tinkle in the empty
  shop, a musk
Of soap and turf and sweets would hit you from the gloom.
  Tobacco.
Baling wire. Twine. And, of course, shelves and pyramids of
  tins.
An old woman would appear from the back — there was a
  sizzling pan in there,
Somewhere, a whiff of eggs and bacon — and ask you what
  you wanted;
Or rather, she wouldn't ask; she would talk about the weather.
  It had rained
That day, but it was looking better. They had just put in the
  spuds.
I had only come to pass the time of day, so I bought a token
  packet of Gold Leaf.

All this time the fry was frying away. Maybe she'd a daughter
  in there
Somewhere, though I hadn't heard the neighbours talk of it;
  if anybody knew,
It would be Horse. Horse kept his ears to the ground.
And he was a great man for current affairs; he owned the only
  TV in the place.
Come dusk he'd set off on his rounds, to tell the whole
  townland the latest
Situation in the Middle East, a mortar bomb attack in
  Mullaghbawn —
The damn things never worked, of course — and so he'd tell
  the story
How in his young day it was very different. Take young Flynn,
  for instance,
Who was ordered to take this bus and smuggle some sticks
  of gelignite

Across the border, into Derry, when the RUC — or was it the
  RIC? —
Got wind of it. The bus was stopped, the peeler stepped on.
  Young Flynn
Took it like a man, of course: he owned up right away. He
  opened the bag
And produced the bomb, his rank and serial number. For all
  the world
Like a pound of sausages. Of course, the thing was, the peeler's
  bike
Had got a puncture, and he didn't know young Flynn from
  Adam. All he wanted
Was to get home for his tea. Flynn was in for seven years
  and learned to speak
The best of Irish. He had thirteen words for a cow in heat;
A word for the third thwart in a boat, the wake of a boat on
  the ebb tide.

He knew the extinct names of insects, flowers, why this place was called

Whatever: *Carrick*, for example, was *a rock*. He was damn right there —

As the man said, *When you buy meat you buy bones, when you buy land you buy stones.*

You'd be hard put to find a square foot in the whole bloody parish

That wasn't thick with flints and pebbles. To this day he could hear the grate

And scrape as the spade struck home, for it reminded him of broken bones:

Digging a graveyard, maybe — or better still, trying to dig a reclaimed tip

Of broken delph and crockery ware — you know that sound that sets your teeth on edge

When the chalk squeaks on the blackboard, or you shovel ashes from the stove?

Master McGinty — he'd be on about McGinty then, and discipline, the capitals

Of South America, Moore's *Melodies*, the Battle of Clontarf, and

Tell me this, an educated man like you: What goes on four legs when it's young,

Two legs when it's grown up, and three legs when it's old? I'd pretend

I didn't know. McGinty's leather strap would come up then, stuffed

With threepenny bits to give it weight and sting. Of course, it never did him

Any harm: *You could take a horse to water but you couldn't make him drink.*

He himself was nearly going on to be a priest.

*And many's the young cub left the school, as wise as when he
came.*

Carrowkeel was where McGinty came from — *Narrow Quarter*,
Flynn explained —
Back before the Troubles, a place that was so mean and
crabbed,
Horse would have it, men were known to eat their dinner
from a drawer.
Which they'd slide shut the minute you'd walk in.
He'd demonstrate this at the kitchen table, hunched and
furtive, squinting
Out the window — past the teetering minarets of rust, down
the hedge-dark aisle —
To where a stranger might appear, a passer-by, or what was
maybe worse,
Someone he knew. Someone who wanted something. Someone
who was hungry.
Of course who should come tottering up the lane that
instant but his brother

Mule. I forgot to mention they were twins. They were as
like two —
No, not peas in a pod, for this is not the time nor the place
to go into
Comparisons, and this is really Horse's story, Horse who —
now I'm getting
Round to it — flew over Dresden in the war. He'd emigrated
first, to
Manchester. Something to do with scrap — redundant mill
machinery,
Giant flywheels, broken looms that would, eventually, be
ships, or aeroplanes.
He said he wore his fingers to the bone.

And so, on impulse, he had joined the RAF. He became a rear
    gunner.
Of all the missions, Dresden broke his heart. It reminded him
    of china.

As he remembered it, long afterwards, he could hear, or
    almost hear
Between the rapid desultory thunderclaps, a thousand tinkling
    echoes —
All across the map of Dresden, store-rooms full of china
    shivered, teetered
And collapsed, an avalanche of porcelain, slushing and
    cascading: cherubs,
Shepherdesses, figurines of Hope and Peace and Victory,
    delicate bone fragments.
He recalled in particular a figure from his childhood, a
    milkmaid
Standing on the mantelpiece. Each night as they knelt down
    for the rosary,
His eyes would wander up to where she seemed to beckon
    to him, smiling,
Offering him, eternally, her pitcher of milk, her mouth of
    rose and cream.

One day, reaching up to hold her yet again, his fingers
    stumbled, and she fell.
He lifted down a biscuit tin, and opened it.
It breathed an antique incense: things like pencils, snuff,
    tobacco.
His war medals. A broken rosary. And there, the milkmaid's
creamy hand, the outstretched
Pitcher of milk, all that survived. Outside, there was a scraping
And a tittering; I knew Mule's step by now, his careful
    drunken weaving

Through the tin-stacks. I might have stayed the night, but
  there's no time
To go back to that now; I could hardly, at any rate, pick up
  the thread.
I wandered out through the steeples of rust, the gate that was
  a broken bed.

Judgement

*The tarred road simmered in a blue haze. The reservoir was
    dry*
*The railway sleepers oozed with creosote. Not a cloud to be
    seen in the sky*

We were sitting at the Camlough halt — Johnny Mickey and
    myself — waiting
For a train that never seemed to come. He was telling me
    this story
Of a Father Clarke, who wanted to do in his dog. A black
    and white terrier.
He says to the servant boy, *Take out that old bitch*, he says,
    and drown her.
Johnny Mickey said the servant boy was Quigley, and now
    that he remembered it,
He'd been arrested by a Sergeant Flynn, for having no bell
    on his bike.
Hardly a hanging crime, you might say. But he was fined
    fifteen shillings.

*The prisoner left the court-room and his step was long and
    slow*
*By day and night he did contrive to fill this sergeant's heart
    with woe*

So there was this auction one day, and Quigley sneaks in the
    back.
A lot of crockery ware came up. Delph bowls. Willow-pattern.
    Chamberpots.
The bidding started at a shilling. Quigley lifts his finger.
    One-and-six.
Everyone pretending not to look at one another. Or to know
    each other.
Nods and winks. A folded *Dundalk Democrat*. Spectacles
    put on and off.

And so on, till he won the bid at fifteen shillings. *Name,*
  please,
Says the auctioneer. *Sergeant Flynn,* says Quigley, *Forkhill*
  Barracks.

For to uphold the letter of the law this sergeant was too
  willing
I took the law upon myself and fined him back his fifteen
  shillings

He rambled on a bit — how this Flynn's people on his
  mother's side
Were McErleans from County Derry, how you could never
  trust
A McErlean. When they hanged young McCorley on the
  bridge of Toome
It was a McErlean who set the whole thing up. That was in
  '98,
But some things never changed. You could trust a dog but
  not a cat.
It was something in their nature, and nature, as they say,
  will out.
The pot would always call the kettle black. He hummed a
  few lines.

Come tender-hearted Christians all attention pay to me
Till I relate and communicate these verses two or three
Concerning of a gallant youth was cut off in his bloom
And died upon the gallows tree near to the town of Toome

Which brought Johnny Mickey back to the priest and the
  terrier bitch.
Quigley, it transpired, had walked the country — Ballinliss
  and Aughaduff,

Slievenacapall, Carnavaddy — looking for a place to drown her.

It was the hottest summer in living memory. Not a cloud to be seen in the sky.

The Cully Water was a trickle. The Tullyallen and the Ummeracam were dry.

Not a breath of wind. Not so much water as would drown a rat. After three days

Quigley and the bitch came back. They were both half-dead with thirst.

He looked her up he looked her down in his heart was ne'er a pang
I'll tell you what says Father Clarke if she won't be drowned she'll hang

Johnny Mickey said that priests had a great way with ropes and knots.

It was one of the tricks that they learned in the seminary. Something to do

With chasubles and albs. In less time than it takes to tell, Father Flynn

had rigged up a noose. They brought the bitch out to the orchard

And strung her up from the crook of an apple tree. And who was passing by

But the poet McCooey. He peeped through a hole in the hedge.

He spotted the two boys at their trade, and this is what he said:

A man with no bell on his bike a man with a single bed
It's hardly any wonder that you'd go off your head
Poor old bitch poor old friend you died without a bark
Sentenced by Johnny Quigley and hung by Father Clarke

Of course, said Johnny Mickey, your man McCooey's long
   since dead.
A white plume of steam appeared around the bend. A long
   lonesome blast.
The tracks began to shimmer and to hum. Our train was
   coming in
And not a minute late. It shivered to a halt. We both got on.
We would pass the crazy map of a dried-up reservoir. A water-
   tower.
We would watch the telegraph lines float up and down, till
   we arrived
At the other end; I would hand Mickey Quigley over to the
   two attendants.

Farewell unto you sweet Drumaul if in you I had stayed
Among the Presbyterians I ne'er would have been betrayed
The gallows tree I ne'er would have seen had I remained
   there
For Dufferin you betrayed me McErlean you set the snare

Belfast Confetti

Suddenly as the riot squad moved in, it was raining
  exclamation marks,
Nuts, bolts, nails, car-keys. A fount of broken type. And the
  explosion
Itself — an asterisk on the map. This hyphenated line, a burst
  of rapid fire . . .
I was trying to complete a sentence in my head, but it kept
  stuttering,
All the alleyways and side-streets blocked with stops and
  colons.

I know this labyrinth so well — Balaclava, Raglan, Inkerman,
  Odessa Street —
Why can't I escape? Every move is punctuated. Crimea
  Street. Dead end again.
A Saracen, Kremlin-2 mesh. Makrolon face-shields. Walkie-
  talkies. What is
My name? Where am I coming from? Where am I going?
  A fusillade of question-marks.

Clearance

The Royal Avenue Hotel collapses under the breaker's
  pendulum:
Zig-zag stairwells, chimney-flues, and a 'thirties mural
Of an elegantly-dressed couple doing what seems to be the
  Tango, in Wedgewood
Blue and white — happy days! Suddenly more sky
Than there used to be. A breeze springs up from nowhere —

There, through a gap in the rubble, a greengrocer's shop
I'd never noticed until now. Or had I passed it yesterday?
  Everything —
Yellow, green and purple — is fresh as paint. Rain glistens on
  the aubergines
And peppers; even from this distance, the potatoes smell of earth.

Linear B

Threading rapidly between crowds on Royal Avenue, reading
Simultaneously, and writing in this black notebook, peering
  through
A cracked lens fixed with Sellotape, his *rendez-vous* is not
  quite *vous*.
But from years of watching, I know the zig-zags circle:
He has been the same place many times, never standing still.

One day I clicked with his staccato walk, and glimpsed the
  open notebook:
Squiggles, dashes, question-marks, dense as the Rosetta stone.
His good eye glittered at me: it was either nonsense, or a
  formula — for
Perpetual motion, the scaffolding of shopping lists, or the
  collapsing city.

Night Patrol

Jerking his head spasmodically as he is penetrated by invisible
  gunfire,
The private wakes to a frieze of pull-outs from *Contact* and
  Men Only.
Sellotape and Blu-Tack. The antiquated plumbing is stuttering
  that he
Is not in Balkan Street or Hooker Street, but in a bunk bed
In the Grand Central Hotel: a room that is a room knocked
  into other rooms.

But the whole Victorian creamy façade has been tossed off
To show the inner-city tubing: cables, sewers, a snarl of
  Portakabins,
Soft-porn shops and carry-outs. A Telstar Taxis depot that is
  a hole
In a breeze-block wall, a wire grille and a voice-box uttering
  gobbledygook.

Campaign

They had questioned him for hours. Who exactly was he?
  And when
He told them, they questioned him again. When they accepted
  who he was, as
Someone not involved, they pulled out his fingernails. Then
They took him to a waste-ground somewhere near the
  Horseshoe Bend, and told him
What he was. They shot him nine times.

A dark umbilicus of smoke was rising from a heap of burning
  tyres.
The bad smell he smelt was the smell of himself. Broken glass
  and knotted Durex.
The knuckles of a face in a nylon stocking. I used to see him
  in the Gladstone Bar,
Drawing pints for strangers, his almost-perfect fingers flecked
  with scum.

Smithfield Market

Sidelong to the arcade, the glassed-in April cloud — fleeting,
  pewter-edged —
Gets lost in shadowed aisles and inlets, branching into
  passages, into cul-de-sacs,
Stalls, compartments, alcoves. Everything unstitched,
  unravelled — mouldy fabric,
Rusted heaps of nuts and bolts, electrical spare parts: the
  ammunition dump
In miniature. Maggots seethe between the ribs and
  corrugations.

Since everything went up in smoke, no entrances, no exits.
But as the charred beams hissed and flickered, I glimpsed a
  map of Belfast
In the ruins: obliterated streets, the faint impression of a key.
Something many-toothed, elaborate, stirred briefly in the
  labyrinth.

Army

The duck patrol is waddling down the odd-numbers side of
    Raglan Street,
The bass-ackwards private at the rear trying not to think of
    a third eye
Being drilled in the back of his head. Fifty-five. They stop.
    The head
Peers round, then leaps the gap of Balaclava Street. He waves
    the body over
One by one. Forty-nine. Cape Street. A gable wall. Garnet
    Street. A gable wall.

Frere Street. Forty-seven. Forty-five-and-a-half. Milan Street.
    A grocer's shop.
They stop. They check their guns. Thirteen. Milton Street.
    An iron lamp-post.
Number One. Ormond Street. *Two ducks in front of a duck
    and two ducks*
Behind a duck, how many ducks? Five? *No. Three.* This
    is not the end.

33333

I was trying to explain to the invisible man behind the wire-
grilled
One-way mirror and squawk-box exactly where it was I
wanted to go, except
I didn't know myself — a number in the Holy Land, Damascus
Street or Cairo?
At any rate in about x amount of minutes, where x is a small
number,
I found myself in the synthetic leopard-skin bucket-seat of a
Ford Zephyr

Gunning through a mesh of ramps, diversions, one-way
systems. We shoot out
Under the glare of the sodium lights along the blank brick
wall of the Gasworks
And I start to ease back: I know this place like the back of
my hand, except
My hand is cut off at the wrist. We stop at an open door I
never knew existed.

Two Winos

Most days you will find this pair reclining on the waste ground
Between Electric Street and Hemp Street, sharing a bottle of
    Drawbridge
British Wine. They stare at isolated clouds, or puffs of steam
    which leak out
From the broken pipes and vents at the back of the Franklin
    Laundry . . .
They converse in snarls and giggles, and they understand each
    other perfectly.

Just now they have entered the giggling phase, though what
    there is
To laugh at, who knows. Unless it was this momentary ray
    of sunlight
That glanced across their patch of crushed coke, broken glass
    and cinders;
And the bottle which had seemed half-empty until then is
    now half-full.

Cocktails

Bombing at about ninety miles an hour with the exhaust
    skittering
The skid-marked pitted tarmac of Kennedy Way, they hit
    the ramp and sailed
Clean over the red-and-white guillotine of the check-point
    and landed
On the M1 flyover, then disappeared before the Brits knew
    what hit them. So
The story went: we were in the Whip and Saddle bar of the
    Europa.

There was talk of someone who was shot nine times and
    lived, and someone else
Had the inside info on the Romper Room. We were trying
    to remember the facts
Behind the Black & Decker case, when someone ordered
    another drink and we entered
The realm of Jabberwocks and Angels' Wings, Widows'
    Kisses, Corpse Revivers.

Travellers

On the waste ground that was Market Street and Verner
    Street, wandering trouserless
Through his personal map — junked refrigerators, cars and
    cookers, anchored
Caravans — the small boy trips over an extended tow-bar,
    picks himself up, giggles
And pisses on a smouldering mound of *Pampers. Sic transit
    gloria mundi* —
This is the exact site, now that I recall it, of Murdock's stables,
    past tense.

Murdock himself moved out to the *Flying Horse* estate some
    years ago. He wanted
To end his days among friends; there were Murdocks in the
    local graveyard.
The long umbilicus of dung between his back yard and
    Downpatrick faded. Belfast
Tore itself apart and patched things up again. Like this. Like
    his extended family.

Snowball

All the signs: beehive hair-do, white handbag, white stilettos,
  split skirt.
An Audi Quattro sidles up in first gear past the loading-bay
  of Tomb Street
GPO — a litter of white plastic cord, a broken whiskey
  bottle —
Then revs away towards the Albert Clock. The heels click
  off — another
Blind date? Like a fish-net stocking, everything is full of
  holes . . .

Arse-about-face, night-shift and the Christmas rush, perfume
  oozing from
Crushed packets — *Blue Grass, Obsession* — and once, in a
  forgotten pigeon-hole,
I woke up to this card stamped 9 August 1910: *Meet me usual
  place & time
Tomorrow — What I have to tell you might not wait —
Yours — Forever — B.*

The Exiles' Club

Every Thursday in the upstairs lounge of the Wollongong
    Bar they make
Themselves at home with Red Heart Stout, Park Drive
    cigarettes and Dunville's whiskey,
A slightly-mouldy batch of soda farls. Eventually, they get
    down to business.
After years they have reconstructed the whole of the Falls
    Road, and now
Are working on the back streets: Lemon, Peel and Omar,
    Balaclava, Alma.

They just about keep up with the news of bombings and
    demolition, and are
Struggling with the finer details: the names and dates carved
    out
On the back bench of the Leavers' Class in Slate Street
    School; the Nemo Café menu;
The effects of the 1941 Blitz, the entire contents of Paddy
    Lavery's pawnshop.

Slate Street School

Back again. Day one. Fingers blue with cold. I joined the
　　lengthening queue.
Roll-call. Then inside: chalk-dust and iced milk, the smell of
　　watered ink.
Roods, perches, acres, ounces, pounds, tons weighed
　　imponderably in the darkening
Air. We had chanted the twelve-times table for the twelfth
　　or thirteenth time
When it began to snow. Chalky numerals shimmered down;
　　we crowded to the window —

*These are the countless souls of purgatory, whose numbers
　　constantly diminish*
*And increase; each flake as it brushes to the ground is yet
　　another soul released.*
And I am the avenging Archangel, stooping over mills and
　　factories and barracks.
I will bury the dark city of Belfast forever under snow: inches,
　　feet, yards, chains, miles.

The Irish for No

Was it a vision, or a waking dream? I heard her voice before
    I saw
What looked like the balcony scene in *Romeo and Juliet*,
    except Romeo
Seemed to have shinned up a pipe and was inside arguing
    with her. The casements
Were wide open and I could see some Japanese-style wall-
    hangings, the dangling
Quotation marks of a yin-yang mobile. *It's got nothing*, she
    was snarling, *nothing*
To do with politics, and, before the bamboo curtain came down,
    That goes for you too!

It was time to turn into the dog's-leg short-cut from Chlorine
    Gardens
Into Cloreen Park, where you might see an *Ulster Says No*
    scrawled on the side
Of the power-block — which immediately reminds me of
    the Eglantine Inn
Just on the corner: on the missing *h* of Cloreen, you might
    say. We were debating,
Bacchus and the pards and me, how to render *The Ulster*
    Bank — the Bank
That Likes to Say Yes into Irish, and whether eglantine was
    alien to Ireland.
I cannot see what flowers are at my feet, when *yes* is the verb
    repeated,
Not exactly yes, but phatic nods and whispers. *The Bank*
    That Answers All
Your Questions, maybe? That Greek portico of Mourne
    granite, dazzling
With promises and feldspar, mirrors you in the Delphic
    black of its windows.

And the bruised pansies of the funeral parlour are dying in
    reversed gold letters,
The long sigh of the afternoon is not yet complete on the
    promontory where the victim,
A corporal in the UDR from Lisbellaw, was last seen having
    driven over half
Of Ulster, a legally-held gun was found and the incidence of
    stress came up
On the headland which shadows Larne Harbour and the
    black pitch of warehouses.
There is a melancholy blast of diesel, a puff of smoke which
    might be black or white.
So the harbour slips away to perilous seas as things remain
    unsolved; we listen
To the *ex cathedra* of the fog-horn, and *drink and leave the
    world unseen* —

What's all this to the Belfast business-man who drilled
Thirteen holes in his head with a Black & Decker? It was
    just a normal morning
When they came. The tennis-court shone with dew or frost,
    a little before dawn.
The border, it seemed, was not yet crossed: the Milky Way
    trailed snowy brambles,
The stars clustered thick as blackberries. They opened the
    door into the dark:
The murmurous haunt of flies on summer eves. Empty jam-jars.
Mish-mash. Hotch-potch. And now you rub your eyes and
    get acquainted with the light
A dust of something reminiscent drowses over the garage
    smell of creosote,
The concrete: blue clouds in porcelain, a paint-brush steeped
    in a chipped cup;

Staples hyphenate a wet cardboard box as the upturned can
    of oil still spills
And the unfed cat toys with the yin-yang of a tennis-ball,
    debating whether *yes* is *no*.

Serial

As the Guinness-like chiaroscuro of the cat settled into the
    quickthorn hedge
I had a feeling I'd been there before: in a black taxi, for
    example, when this bullet
Drilled an invisible bee-line through the open window and
    knocked a chip
Off the Scotch sandstone façade of the Falls Road Library.
    Everybody ducked
To miss the already-dead split-second; the obvious soldier
    relaxed back into
His Guinness-and-tan uniform, since to hear the shot is to
    know you are alive.

It is this lapse of time which gives the film its serial quality:
    the next
Episode is about the giant statue of the newly-renovated
    Carson, verdigris becoming
Bronze. It is suggested that it might be camouflage — as
    glossed on
In the SF novels of W. D. Flackes, particularly in his novel,
    *The X
People.* And so in the words of another commentator, *the
    future is only today
Fading into the past* — drawing, perhaps, a retrospective
    dotted line on the map

For from here the border makes a peninsula of the South,
    especially in the shallows
Of Lough Erne, where so much land is so much water
    anyway. And, since the Ormsby
Room in Lakeland still remains un-named, they are thinking
    of calling it
Something else: not a name, but the name of a place. Blacklion,
    for instance.

*The Blacklion Room has a certain sort of armorial flavour
which would suit*
The tourist junkets, the loops and spirals of an Irish dancing
costume.

Waterfowlers in ulsters, mackintoshes, flak jackets, tank-tops,
wade in
Through the rushes and ignore the German fishermen trapped
in the caves of Boho.
The water-level is neither here nor there: as they say, *it's
making up its mind*
To rain, the grey brainy mass of the clouds becoming cabbages,
since a foot patrol
Has just gone over to the other side: you can identify them
by the black markings
On their cheeks, the fact that it is winter and the hedges are
bare.

These errors of reading are not the only difference between
us and them
Though the shibboleths are *lingua franca*, since German
became current.
As for Irish, it was too identifiable as foreign: a museum
where the stuffed
Wolfhound was just as native as the Shell tiger — I am hunting
with a telephoto
Fish-eye, shooting, as they say, some footage. The crackly
static
Of the portable still gives some news, though, in between
the magazines:

I am hearing a lot, for example, of this campaign to save the
English frog.
Refrigerators stocked with spawn are humming quietly in
wait; the light

Goes off with a click as you shut the door. The freezing
    dark suggests
That they are dying anyway, perplexed by their bi-focal
    vision, as next week,
Or the last week, are the same, and nothing can be justified
As the independent eye of the chameleon sees blue as green.

Asylum

The first indication was this repeated tic, the latch jigging
and clicking
As he rehearsed the possibility of entering, or opening. Maybe
It was a knock, a question; Uncle John was not all there. Yet
he had
His father's eyes, his mother's nose; and I myself, according
to my mother,
Had his mouth. I would imagine speaking for him sometimes.
He had
A second cousin's hands, or a cousin's twice removed, an
uncle's way of walking:
In other words, he was himself. So he might walk in this
very minute, or turn
His back on us to contemplate the yellow brick edgings of
the bricked-in
Windows of the mill wall opposite. He seemed to see things
that we didn't
See: cloud-shadow eddying and swirling round a manhole;
the bits of grit
That glittered at the edges; individual as dirt, the dog-leg walk
of a dog
As it followed its nose from one side of the street to the other.
His ears
Might prick to the clatter of an empty tin kicked down an
entry,
Diminishing the yelps of children as their skipping rope became
a blur,
Then slowed and stopped, then whipped back up again, the
up-hill down-dale
Quickening pulse of a cardiograph. We watched him hover
and dilate
In the frosted glass. Someone would get up; he would retreat.
An electric
Yellow bakery van hummed by; he sniffed the air. A car
backfired.

Like the fast-forward or the rewind button, everything is
  going far too
Fast, though we might know precisely, having heard it all
  before for real,
What is going on, like that climactic moment of a rounded,
  oratorical
Gesture, practised in the mirror till it seemed completely
  unfamiliar:
The hyped-up, ninety-to-the-dozen commentary that
  illustrates, in retrospect,
The split-second when a goal is scored; the laid-back, bit-
  by-bit analysis
As we take in every slowed-down motion of the replay. We
  are looking
For a piece we know is there, amongst the clutter and the glug
  of bottles,
Whispering, the chink of loose change, the unfamiliar voices
  that are us
And cloud our hearing. The repeated melancholic parp of a
  car-horn
Eventually has heralded the moment: now we know what's
  coming next, the voice
Hoarsened by the second-generation tape, the echo of a
  nearly-empty dusty
Concert-hall, illuminated, we imagine, by the voice, one
  shaft of fitful sunlight
That retreated almost instantly to a nimbo-cumulus —
  gold-edged, slate-blue,
Glimmering between its cup and lip — imponderably weighing
  on the skylight.
A yellow bakery van hums by. There is a lull, and then a car
  backfires.

It's getting nearer now, that out-of-focus look he had: a
  wall-eye

With its yellowed white, the confused rainbow of the iris
   weeping unpredictably.
The tortoise-shell frame had one missing lens. Why they
   were bi-focals
I don't know; he didn't read. Spinning yarns was more his
   line, always something
Off the top of his head. Or he might sing a song: perhaps
   I'm going down the town
*And I know who's going with me. I have a wee boy of my
   own, and his name is —*
Here he'd mention my name, which was almost my name;
   half of it, at least,
Was right. All this while he champed, between gulps of tea,
   two thick buttered
Doorsteps of a *Peter Pan* loaf, and cast his eye on the yellowed
   pages
Of an *Old Moore's Almanac* for 1948, the year, in fact, that I
   was born.
Storms this month, I see; hurricanes and thunder . . . the almanac
   was upside down,
But sure enough, just then, above the smoke-stack of the mill
   on up the street,
I caught a dark umbilicus of cloud, a momentary flash. Rain
   pattered on the window.
A yellow bakery van went by; he sniffed the ozone. A car
   backfired.

You can tell that this was all some time ago, although it does
   repeat itself.
On this particular day, my other uncle, Pat, had just come in
   from work.
He plunked two loaves down on the table. A doughy-sour
   inveterate smell
Breathed out from him, and as he lifted off the white cloud
   of his cap, it sparked off

The authoritative onset of this other, needle-in-the-haystack
   day that I
Began with. That ratchety delay with which the clock is poised,
   conjugating
All its tensed-up coils and springs: rain pattered on the
   window. An electric
Yellow bakery van whirred off. A car backfired. Someone
   seemed to get up very
Slowly. A dog was barking. The car backfired again. Everything was getting faster

And the door bursts open. He is babbling, stammering,
   contractions
Getting nearer, nearer, all the blips run into one another till
   they are
A wave, a wall: *They said to push, she pushed, they said to
   shut her mouth,*
*She pushed, they said to keep her head down, and she pushed
   once more* —
The wave has almost broken — *more, they said*: a lock of
   hair, a bald patch,
Hair again. Flecks of blood and foam. He cannot get it all
   out fast enough.

Afterwards, a lull. He sits up and he takes a cup of tea, a slice
   of toast.
He is himself again, though I can see myself in him. *I
   remember very well*, he says,
When you were born; oh yes, thunder, hurricanes; and as I
   see the bruised
Posthumous violet of his face, I hear him talk about the shape
   of this particular
Cloud he saw last week, or this dog he'd noticed last week,
   which he'd imitate,

Panting, slabbering and heaving as it lolled about the margins
   of the new estate —
Nettles, yellow chickweed, piss-the-beds — sniffing,
   wagging, following itself
Back through that remembered day of complex perfume, a
   trail of moments
Dislocated, then located. This dog. That bitch. There is a
   long-forgotten
Whimper, a groan of joy as it discovers home: a creosoted
   hutch, a bowl,
The acrid spoor of something that was human.

Patchwork

It was only just this minute that I noticed the perfectly triangular
Barbed wire rip in the sleeve of my shirt, and wondered where I'd got it.
I'd crossed no fences that I knew about. Then it struck me: an almost identical
Tear in my new white Sunday shirt, when I was six. My mother, after her initial
Nagging, stitched it up. But you can never make a perfect job on tears like that.
Eventually she cut it up for handkerchiefs: six neatly-hemmed squares.
Snags of greyish wool remind me of the mountain that we climbed that day —
Nearly at the summit, we could see the map of Belfast. My father stopped
For a cigarette, and pointed out the landmarks: Gallaher's tobacco factory,
Clonard Monastery, the invisible speck of our house, lost in all the rows
And terraces and furrows, like this one sheep that's strayed into the rags
And bandages that flock the holy well. A little stack of ball-point pens,
Some broken spectacles, a walking-stick, two hearing-aids: prayers
Repeated and repeated until granted.
                                        So when I saw, last week, the crucifix
Ear-ring dangling from the right ear of this young Charismatic
Christian fiddle-player, I could not help but think of beads, beads
Told over and over — like my father's rosary of olive stones from

Mount Olive, I think, that he had thumbed and fingered so
   much, the decades
Missed a pip or two. The cross itself was ebony and silver,
   just like
This young girl's, that swung and tinkled like a thurible. She
   was playing
The Teetotaller. Someone had to buy a drink just then, of
   course: a pint of Harp,
Four pints of stout, two Paddy whiskies, and a bottle of
   Lucozade — the baby
Version, not the ones you get in hospital, wrapped in crackling
   see-through
Cellophane. You remember how you held it to the light, and
   light shone through?
The opposite of Polaroids, really, the world filmed in dazzling
   sunshine:
A quite unremarkable day of mist and drizzle. The rainy hush
   of traffic,
Muted car-horns, a dog making a dog-leg walk across a zebra
   crossing . . .
As the lights changed from red to green and back to red again
I fingered the eighteen stitches in the puckered mouth of my
   appendicectomy.

The doctor's waiting room, now that I remember it, had a
   print of *The Angelus*
Above the fireplace; sometimes, waiting for the buzzer, I'd
   hear the Angelus
Itself boom out from St Peter's. With only two or three
   deliberate steps
I could escape into the frame, unnoticed by the peasant and
   his wife. I'd vanish
Into sepia. The last shivering bell would die on the wind.

I was in the surgery. Stainless steel and hypodermics glinted
on the shelves.
Now I saw my mother: the needle shone between her thumb
and finger, stitching,
Darning, mending: the woolly callous on a sock, the unravelled
jumper
That became a scarf. I held my arms at arms' length as she
wound and wound:
The tick-tack of the knitting needles made a cable-knit pullover.
Come Christmas morning I would wear it, with a new white
shirt unpinned
From its cardboard stiffener.
                                        I shivered at the touch of cold
white linen —
A mild shock, as if, when almost sleeping, you'd dreamt
you'd fallen
Suddenly, and realised now, you were awake: the curtains
fluttered
In the breeze across the open window, exactly as they had
before. Everything
Was back to normal. Outside, the noise of children playing:
a tin can kicked
Across a tarred road, the whip-whop of a skipping-rope,
singing —
*Poor Toby is dead and he lies in his grave, lies in his grave,
lies in his grave . . .*
So, the nicotine-stained bone buttons on my father's melodeon
clicked
And ticked as he wheezed his way through *Oft in the Stilly
Night* — or,
For that matter, *Nearer My God to Thee*, which he'd play on
Sundays, just before
He went to see my granny, after Mass. Sometimes she'd be
sick — *another*

Clean shirt'll do me — and we'd climb the narrow stair to
    where she lay, buried
Beneath the patchwork quilt.
                        It took me twenty years to make
    that quilt —
I'm speaking for her, now — and, *your father's stitched into*
    that quilt,
Your uncles and your aunts. She'd take a sip from the baby
    Power's
On the bedside table. *Anything that came to hand, a bit of*
    cotton print,
A poplin tie: I snipped them all up. I could see her working
    in the gloom,
The shadow of the quilt draped round her knees. A needle
    shone between
Her thumb and finger. Minutes, hours of stitches threaded
    patiently; my father
Tugged at her, a stitch went wrong; she started up again. *You*
    drink your tea
Just like your father: two sups and a gulp: and so, I'd see a
    mirror image
Raise the cup and take two sips, and swallow, or place my cup
    exactly on
The brown ring stain on the white damask tablecloth.
                                    Davy's
    gone to England,
Rosie to America; who'll be next, I don't know. Yet they all
    came back.
I'd hardly know them now. The last time I saw them all
    together, was
The funeral. As the Rosary was said, I noticed how my father
    handled the invisible
Bead on the last decade: a gesture he'd repeat again at the
    graveside.

A shower of hail: far away, up on the mountain, a cloud of
    sheep had scattered
In the Hatchet Field. *The stitches show in everything I've
    made,* she'd say —
The quilt was meant for someone's wedding, but it never got
    that far.
And some one of us has it now, though who exactly I don't
    know.

Turn Again

There is a map of the city which shows the bridge that was
   never built.
A map which shows the bridge that collapsed; the streets
   that never existed.
Ireland's Entry, Elbow Lane, Weigh-House Lane, Back Lane,
   Stone-Cutter's Entry —
Today's plan is already yesterday's — the streets that were
   there are gone.
And the shape of the jails cannot be shown for security reasons.

The linen backing is falling apart — the Falls Road hangs by
   a thread.
When someone asks me where I live, I remember where I
   used to live.
Someone asks me for directions, and I think again. I turn into
A side-street to try to throw off my shadow, and history is
   changed.

Loaf

I chewed it over, this whiff I got just now, but trying to pin
  down
That aroma — yeast, salt, flour, water — is like writing on the
  waxed sleeve
That it's wrapped in: the nib keeps skidding off. Or the ink
  won't take. Blue-black
Quink is what I used then. I liked the in-between-ness of it,
  neither
One thing nor the other. A *Conway Stewart* fountain-pen,
  blue-ish green
Mock tortoiseshell . . . the lever sticking sometimes in the
  quick of my thumb,
I'd fill her up: a contented slurp like the bread you use to sup
  up
Soup. McWatters' pan loaf, some said, was like blotting-
  paper: I thought of
Leonardo's diary, or a mirror code ending with, *Eat this.*
Well, some people *like* blotting-paper. I used to eat chalk
  myself. Raw
Flour, oatmeal. Paper. A vitamin deficiency? The corners of
My books weren't dog-eared, they were chewed. But neatly
  chewed, like the thumb-index
Of a dictionary. I ate my way from *A* to *Z*, the list of weights
And measures. So now I'm in McWatters' flour-loft. Grains,
  pecks and bushels:

So much raw material. *I* was raw. This was a summer job,
  not real
Work. Myself and this other skiver, we mostly talked of this
  and that —
Cigarettes and whiskey — between whatever it was we were
  supposed
To do. Joe reckoned that Jameson's *Three Swallows* was hard
  to beat

Though you could make a case for their *Robin Redbreast* or
Power's *Gold Label*.
One had the edge the others didn't, though you couldn't quite
describe it.
Like Gallaher's *Greens*: dry, smoky, biting. He had this bebop
hairstyle —
Bee-bap, as they say in Belfast, a golden fuzz pricked up
from the scalp —
And he'd done time at one time or another for some petty
crime. Theft?
Jiggery-pokery. Night-shifts. The kind of fly moves that get
you caught.
And as it happened, he was between times just then, like me
between terms.

It seemed the Health Inspectors were due in a while, so we
were given
Galvanized buckets, sponges, those mops with the head of
an albino
Golliwog. The place breathed gunge and grease, the steamy
damp of baking bread.
So as I say, we talked: football, drink, girls, horses, though I
didn't know
Much on any of these scores. They were clouds on the blue
of the future.
Walking the slippery catwalk from one bake-room to the next —
like Dante's
Inferno, the midnight glare of ovens, a repeated doughy slap
Of moulds being filled — we'd think of the cool of the loo
or a lunchtime pint.
The bitter edge of Guinness would cut through the bread
and oxtail soup
Till bread and soup and stout became all one. We would talk
with our mouths full.

Then back to *Ajax* and *Domestos*, the Augean pandemonium.
Or sorting out spoiled loaves for pig-feed — waxed wrappers
    in one bag, sliced pan
In the other; the pigs, it seemed, were particular. At other
    times,
Stacking up empty flour-sacks: cloudy caesurae floating one
    on top
Of one another, the print so faded we could barely read the
    text;
That choked-up weave meant nothing much but passing time.
    Expanding moments,
Watching dough rise, the stretch-marks lost in the enormous
    puff-ball — *Is this*
The snow that was so bright last year?
                                    We worked slowly
        through the levels, till
We found ourselves at last in No. 2 loft, high above the
    racket.
My last week. As for him, he didn't know. Muffled by
    forgotten drifts
Of flour, I was thinking of the future, he was buried in the
    past.
This move he'd worked, this girl he'd known. Everything
    stored away in cells.
Pent-up honey talk oozed out of him, while I sang, *Che sarà
sarà.*

He asked if I'd remember him. We wrote our names on the
    snowed-up panes.
The date, the names of girls, hearts and arrows. We made up
    affairs between
The bakers and the packers — bread and paper — then we
    wiped it all clean.

The glass shone for the first time in years. We were staring out
  the window
At the end of summer. Aeroplanes flew by at intervals, going
  elsewhere:
Tiny specks, the white lines of their past already fuzzing up
  the blue.

Snow

A white dot flicked back and forth across the bay window:
not
A table-tennis ball, but 'ping-pong', since this is happening
in another era,
The extended leaves of the dining-table — scratched mahogany
veneer —
Suggesting many such encounters, or time passing: the
celluloid diminuendo
As it bounces off into a corner and ticks to an incorrigible
stop.
I pick it up days later, trying to get that pallor right: it's
neither ivory
Nor milk. Chalk is better; and there's a hint of pearl,
translucent
Lurking just behind opaque. I broke open the husk so many
times
And always found it empty; the pith was a wordless bubble.

Though there's nothing in the thing itself, bits of it come
back unbidden,
Playing in the archaic dusk till the white blip became invisible.
Just as, the other day, I felt the tacky pimples of a ping-pong
bat
When the bank-clerk counted out my money with her rubber
thimble, and knew
The black was bleeding into red. Her face was snow and roses
just behind
The bullet-proof glass: I couldn't touch her if I tried. I
crumpled up the chit —
No use in keeping what you haven't got — and took a stroll
to Ross's auction.
There was this 'thirties scuffed leather sofa I wanted to
make a bid for.
Gestures, prices: soundlessly collateral in the murmuring
room.

I won't say what I paid for it: anything's too much when
  you have nothing.
But in the dark recesses underneath the cushions I found
  myself kneeling
As decades of the Rosary dragged by, the slack of years ago
  hauled up
Bead by bead; and with them, all the haberdashery of loss —
  cuff buttons,
Broken ball-point pens and fluff, old pennies, pins and
  needles, and yes,
A ping-pong ball. I cupped it in my hands like a crystal,
  seeing not
The future, but a shadowed parlour just before the blinds
  are drawn. Someone
Has put up two trestles. Handshakes all round, nods and
  whispers.
Roses are brought in, and suddenly, white confetti seethes
  against the window.

Ambition

*'I did not allow myself to think of ultimate escape . . .
one step at a time was enough.'*
— John Buchan, *Mr Standfast*

Now I've climbed this far, it's time to look back. But smoke
obscures
The panorama from the Mountain Loney spring. The city
and the mountain are on fire.
My mouth's still stinging from the cold sharp shock of water —
a winter taste
In summer — but my father's wandered off somewhere. I
can't seem to find him.
We'd been smoking 'coffin nails', and he'd been talking of
his time inside, how
Matches were that scarce, you'd have to split them four ways
with your thumb-nail;
And seven cigarette ends made a cigarette. *Keep a thing for
seven years,*
You'll always find a use for it, he follows in the same breath
. . . it reminds me
Of the saint who, when he had his head cut off, picked up
his head, and walked
With it for seven miles. And the wise man said, *The distance
doesn't matter,*
It's the first step that was difficult.

Any journey's like that — *the first step of your life*, my father
interrupts —
Though often you take one step forward, two steps back. For
if time is a road,
It's fraught with ramps and dog-legs, switchbacks and
spaghetti; here and there,
The dual carriageway becomes a one-track, backward mind.
And bits of the landscape

Keep recurring: it seems as if I've watched the same suburban
    tennis match
For hours, and heard, at ever less-surprising intervals, the
    applause of pigeons
Bursting from a loft. Or the issue is not yet decided, as the
    desultory handclaps
Turn to rain. The window that my nose is pressed against is
    breathed-on, giving
Everything a sfumato air. I keep drawing faces on it, or prac-
    tising my signature.

And if time is a road, then you're checked again and again
By a mobile checkpoint. One soldier holds a gun to your
    head. Another soldier
Asks you questions, and another checks the information on
    the head computer.
Your name. Your brothers' names. Your father's name. His
    occupation. As if
The one they're looking for is not you, but it might be you.
    Looks like you
Or smells like you. And suddenly, the posthumous aroma
    of an empty canvas
Postman's sack — twine, ink, dead letters — wafts out from
    the soldiers'
Sodden khaki. It's obvious they're bored: one of them is watch-
    ing Wimbledon
On one of those postage-stamp-sized TV screens. *Of course,
    the proper shot,*
An unseen talking head intones, *should have been the lob.* He's
    using words like
Angled, volley, smash and *strategy.* Someone is *fighting a losing
    battle.*
Isn't that the way, that someone tells you what you should
    have done, when

You've just done the opposite? *Did you give the orders for
this man's death?*
On the contrary, the accused replies, as if he'd ordered birth
or resurrection.
Though *one nail drives out another*, as my father says.

And my father should have known better than to tamper
with Her Majesty's
Royal Mail — or was it His, then? His humour was to take
an Irish ha'penny
With the harp on the flip side, and frank a letter with it. Some
people didn't
See the joke; they'd always thought him a Republican. He
was reported,
Laid off for a month. Which is why he never got promoted. So
one story goes.
The other is a war-time one, where he's supposed to go to
England
For a training course, but doesn't, seeing he doesn't want to
get conscripted.
My mother's version is, he lacked ambition. He was too content
to stay
In one place. He liked things as they were . . . *perfect touch,
perfect timing, perfect
Accuracy*: the commentary has just nudged me back a little,
as I manage
To take in the action replay. There's a tiny puff of chalk, as
the ball skids off
The line, like someone might be firing in slow motion, far
away: that otherwise
Unnoticeable faint cloud on the summer blue, which makes
the sky around it
All the more intense and fragile.

It's nearer to a winter blue. A zig-zag track of footsteps is imprinted
On the frosted tennis-court: it looks as if the Disappeared One rose before
First light, and stalked from one side of the wire cage to the other, off
Into the glinting laurels. No armed wing has yet proclaimed responsibility:
One hand washes the other, says my father, as sure as *one funeral makes many*.
For the present is a tit-for-tat campaign, exchanging *now* for *then*,
The Christmas post of Christmas Past, the black armband of the temporary man;
The insignia have mourned already for this casual preserve. Threading
Through the early morning suburbs and the monkey-puzzle trees, a smell of coffee lingers,
Imprisoned in the air like wisps of orange peel in marmalade; and sleigh-bell music
Tinkles on the radio, like ice cubes in a summer drink. I think I'm starting, now,
To know the street map with my feet, just like my father.

God never shuts one door, said my father, *but he opens up another*; and then,
I walked the iron catwalk naked in the freezing cold: he's back into his time
As internee, the humiliation of the weekly bath. It was seven weeks before
He was released: it was his younger brother they were after all the time.
God never opens one door, but he shuts another: my uncle was inside for seven years.

At his funeral, they said how much I looked like him: I've
    got his smoker's cough,
At any rate. And now my father's told to cut down on the
    cigarettes, he smokes
Them three or four puffs at a time. Stubs them out and lights
    them, seven times.
I found him yesterday a hundred yards ahead of me, struggling,
    as the blazing
Summer hauled him one step at a time into a freezing furnace.
    And with each step
He aged. As I closed in on him, he coughed. I coughed. He
    stopped and turned,
Made two steps back towards me, and I took one step forward.

Queen's Gambit

A Remote Handling Equipment (Tracked) Explosive
    Ordnance Disposal unit — *Wheelbarrow*,
For short — is whirring and ticking towards the Ford
    Sierrra parked in Tomb Street,

Its robotic arm extended indirectly towards this close-up of
    a soldier. He's wearing
An M69 flak jacket, Dr Marten boots and non-regulation
    skiing gloves.

Another soldier, armed with Self-loading Rifle, squats
    beneath a spray-gunned
Flourish of graffiti: *The Provos Are Fighting For You.*
    Remember It. Brits Out.

Now they're seen together leaning against the façade of a
    chemist's shop,
Admiring — so it would appear — the cardboard ad for
    Wilkinson Sword razor blades.

So much, they're now in the interior: a gauzy, pinkish smell
    of soap and sticking-
Plaster, through which they spit word-bubbles at the white-
    coated girl assistant.

Much of this is unintelligible, blotted out by stars and
    asterisks
Just as the street outside is splattered with bits of corrugated
    iron and confetti.

Her slightly antiseptic perfume is a reminiscent *je-ne-sais-*
    quoi
Glimpsed through Pear's Soap, an orange-sepia zest of coal-
    tar —

It's that *moiré* light from the bathroom window, or a body
    seen behind
The shower-curtain, holding a Champagne telephone — the
    colour, not the drink,

Though it gives off a perceptible hiss. And the continuous
    background
Rumble is a string of *M*s and *R*s, expanding and contracting

To reveal the windswept starry night, through which a
    helicopter trawls
Its searchlight. Out there, on the ground, there's a spoor of
    Army boots;

Dogs are following their noses, and terrorists are contem-
    plating
Terror, a glittering, tilted view of mercury, while the assistant
    slithers

Into something more comfortable: jeans, a combat jacket,
    Doc Martens boots;
Then weighs the confidential dumb-bell of the telephone.
    She pushes buttons:

Zero Eight Double Zero. Then the number of the Beast, the
    number of the Beast
Turned upside-down: Six Six Six, Nine Nine Nine . . .

～

The ambient light of yesterday is amplified by talk of might-
    have-beens,
Making 69 — the year — look like quotation marks,
    commentators commenting on

The flash-point of the current Trouble, though there's any
    God's amount
Of Nines and Sixes: 1916, 1690, The Nine Hundred Years'
    War, whatever.

Or maybe we can go back to the Year Dot, the nebulous
    expanding brain-wave
Of the Big Bang, releasing us and It and everything into
    oblivion;

It's so hard to remember, and so easy to forget the casualty
    list —
Like the names on a school desk, carved into one another till
    they're indecipherable.

It's that frottage effect again: the paper that you're scribbling
    on is grained
And blackened, till the pencil-lead snaps off, in a valley of
    the broken alphabet

And the streets are a bad photostat grey: the ink comes off
    on your hand.
With so many foldings and unfoldings, whole segments of
    the map have fallen off.

It's not unlike the missing reel in the film, the blank screen
    jittering
With numerals and flak, till the picture jumps back — a bit
    out of sync,

As soldiers A and B and others of the lettered regiment discuss
    the mission
In their disembodied voices. Only the crackly Pye Pocketfone
    sounds real,

A bee-in-the-biscuit-tin buzzing number codes and decibels.
  They're in the belly
Of a Saracen called 'Felix', the cartoon cat they've taken as a
  mascot:

It's all the go, here, changing something into something else,
  like rhyming
Kampuchea with Cambodia. It's why Mickey Mouse wears
  those little white gloves —

Claws are too much like a mouse. And if the animals are
  trying to be people,
Vice versa is the case as well. Take 'Mad Dog' Reilly, for
  example, who

This instant is proceeding to the rendezvous. A gunman, he
  isn't yet; the rod
Is stashed elsewhere, somewhere in a mental block of dog-leg
  turns and cul-de-sacs.

He sniffs his hand, an antiseptic tang that momentarily
  brings back
The creak of a starched coat crushed against his double-
  breasted gaberdine.

~

After the recorded message, the bleep announces a magnetic
  silence
Towards which she's drawn as conspirator, as towards a
  confessional, whispering

What she knows into the wire-grilled darkness: names,
  dates, places;
More especially, a future venue, Tomb Street GPO.

She wants the slate wiped clean, *Flash* or *Ajax* cutting a
    bright swathe
Through a murky kitchen floor, transforming it into a
    gleaming checkerboard.

Tiles of black and white on which the regiments of pawns
    move ponderously,
Bishops take diagonals, and the Queen sees dazzling lines
    of power.

Or, putting it another way, Operation 'Mad Dog', as it's
    known now,
Is the sketch that's taking shape on the Army HQ black-
    board, chalky ghosts

Behind the present, showing what was contemplated and
    rubbed out, Plan A
Becoming X or Y; interlocked, curved arrows of the mortgaged
    future.

The raffia waste-paper bin is full of crumpled drafts and
    cigarette butts,
And ash has seeped through to the carpet. There's a smell of
    peeled oranges.

But the Unknown Factor, somewhat like the Unknown
    Soldier, has yet to take
The witness box. As someone spills a cup of tea on a discarded
    Irish News

A minor item bleeds through from another page, blurring
    the main story.
It's difficult to pick up without the whole thing coming apart
    in your hands,

But basically it invokes this bunch of cowboys, who,
    unbeknownst to us all,
Have jumped on board a Ford Sierra, bound for You-Know-
    Where.

They're Ordinary Criminals: you know them by the dollar
    signs that shiver
In their eyes, a notion that they're going to hit the jackpot
    of the GPO.

Unbeknownst to themselves, they'll be picked up in the
    amplified light
Of a Telescope Starlight II Night Observation Device
    (NOD) — *Noddy*, for short,

But not before the stoolie-pigeon spool is reeled back;
    amplified,
Its querulous troughs and peaks map out a different curve of
    probability.

❧

My newly-lowered ears in the barber's mirror were starting
    to take on a furtive look.
A prison cut — my face seemed Born Again — but then, I'd
    asked for *short*.

And I've this problem, talking to a man whose mouth is a
    reflection.
I tend to think the words will come out backwards, so I'm
    saying nothing.

And then, says he — he's staring straight into my eyes, the
    scissors poised —
It seems they think they're just about to nail your man O'Reilly

*When a bunch of hoods pulls up in a Ford Sierra and jumps
  out with the sawn-off*
*Shotguns, plastic masks they must have got in Elliot's — Mickey
  Mouse, Donald Duck*

*And Pluto — too much watching TV, if you ask me — so of
  course the Brits let go*
With everything. He snips at my right ear. *But now hear this:*

*This Post Office van bombs out from Tomb Street loading
  bay, its side door open*
*And they've got this effing Gatling gun or something going
  full blast —*

*Dot, dot, dot, dot — and the Brits are all shot up — could you
  move your head a bit —*
*Right — so the Mad Dog, he jumps in the back and him and
  the boys are off like a shot.*

*So what do you think? It looks to me, it was a set-up job,
  though who exactly*
*Was set up, God only knows. You can see it for yourself —
  they've been checking out*

*That Ford Sierra for the past two hours, just as soon as it was
  light.*
*Seems they think the Disney characters were in on it. If you
  ask me,*

*With these confidential telephones, you never know who's doing
  who, or why.*
*Better to keep your mouth shut, that's what I say. Haircut
  OK, sir?*

He held a mirror to my neck. I nodded. He shook out the cloth, and curls
And snippets writhed like commas on the chessboard tiles. Now that I could see

Myself without the hair and beard, I looked like someone else. He brushed
My shoulders, and I left him to a row of empty mirrors, sweeping up

The fallen swathes. Turning into Tomb Street, I began to feel a new man.
Perfume breathed from somewhere, opening avenues of love, or something *déjà vu*.

Last Orders

Squeeze the buzzer on the steel mesh gate like a trigger, but
It's someone else who has you in their sights. Click. It opens.
  Like electronic
Russian roulette, since you never know for sure who's who,
  or what
You're walking into. I, for instance, could be anybody. Though
  I'm told
Taig's written on my face. See me, would *I* trust appearances?

Inside a sudden lull. The barman lolls his head at us. We order
  Harp —
Seems safe enough, everybody drinks it. As someone looks
  daggers at us
From the *Bushmills* mirror, a penny drops: how simple it
  would be for someone
Like ourselves to walk in and blow the whole place, and
  ourselves, to Kingdom Come.

Hairline Crack

It could have been or might have been. Everything Provisional
    and Sticky,
Daily splits and splinters at the drop of a hat or a principle —
The right hand wouldn't even know it was the right hand;
    some would claim it
As the left. If only this, if only that, if only pigs could fly.
Someone decides, hawk or dove. Ambushes are sprung. Velvet
    fist. Iron glove.

It was on the stroke of midnight by the luminous dial of the
    clock
When this woman, caught in crossfire, stooped for the dash-
    board cigarette lighter.
In that instant, a bullet neatly parted her permanent wave.
    So now
She tells the story, how a cigarette made all the odds. Between
    life. And death.

Bloody Hand

Your man, says the Man, *will walk into the bar like this* —
    here his fingers
Mimic a pair of legs, one stiff at the knee — *so you'll know
    exactly*
What to do. He sticks a finger to his head. Pretend it's child's
    play —
The hand might be a horse's mouth, a rabbit or a dog. Five
    handclaps.
Walls have ears: the shadows you throw are the shadows you
    try to throw off.

I snuffed out the candle between finger and thumb. Was it
    the left hand
Hacked off at the wrist and thrown to the shores of Ulster?
    Did Ulster
Exist? Or the Right Hand of God, saying *Stop* to this and *No*
    to that?
My thumb is the hammer of a gun. The thumb goes up. The
    thumb goes down.

Jump Leads

As the eggbeater spy in the sky flickered overhead, the TV
    developed a facial tic
Or as it turned out, the protesters had handcuffed them-
    selves to the studio lights.
Muffled off-camera, shouts of *No*. As I tried to lip-read the
    talking head
An arms cache came up, magazines laid out like a tray of
    wedding rings.
The bomb-disposal expert whose face was in shadow for
    security reasons

Had started very young by taking a torch apart at Christmas
    to see what made it tick.
Everything went dark. The killers escaped in a red Fiesta
    according to sources.
Talking, said the Bishop, is better than killing. Just before
    the Weather
The victim is his wedding photograph. He's been spattered
    with confetti.

Yes

I'm drinking in the 7-Up bottle-green eyes of the barmaid
On the Enterprise express — bottles and glasses clinking each
   other —
When the train slows with a noise like Schweppes and halts
   just outside Dundalk.
Not that unwontedly, since we're no strangers to the border
   bomb.
As the Belfast accent of the tannoy tells us what is happening

I'm about to quote from Basho's *The Narrow Road to the
   Deep North* —
*Blossoming mushroom: from some unknown tree a leaf has
   stuck to it* —
When it goes off and we're thrown out of kilter. My mouth
   is full
Of broken glass and quinine as everything reverses South.

The Mouth

There was this head had this mouth he kept shooting off.
  Unfortunately.
It could have been worse for us than it was for him.
  Provisionally.
But since nothing in this world is certain and you don't
  know who hears what
We thought it was time he bit off more than he could chew.
  Literally.
By the time he is found there'll be nothing much left to tell
  who he was.

But of course some clever dick from the 'Forscenic Lab'
  reconstructs
Him, what he used to be — not from his actual teeth, not
  his fingerprints,
But from the core — the toothmarks of the first and last bite
  he'd taken of
This sour apple. But then we would have told them anyway.
  Publicity.

Night Out

Every Thursday night when we press the brass button on
    the galvanized wire mesh gate
A figure appears momentarily at the end of the strip-lit
    concrete passageway,
Then disappears. The gate squeaks open, slams shut almost
    instantly behind us.
Then through the semi-opaque heavy-duty polythene swing
    doors they might have taken
From a hospital. At the bar, we get the once-over once again.

Seven whiskeys later, the band is launching into *Four Green
    Fields.*
From somewhere out beyond the breeze-block walls we get
    a broken rhythm
Of machine-gun fire. A ragged chorus. So the sentence of
    the night
Is punctuated through and through by rounds of drink, of
    bullets, of applause.

Jawbox

What looks to us like a crackly newsreel, the picture
  jumping with flak,
Was clear as day, once. But that's taken as read, since this is a
  'quotation'
In the main text of the film, which begins with someone
  flicking open
The glossy pages of a *Homes and Gardens* kitchen supplement:
  Sink or Swim, the caption
Says, *The Belfast sink combines old-fashioned charm with
  tried and tested
Practicality* . . . 'Why *Belfast*?', the character begins to ponder —
  he puts the accent
On the *fast*, as if the name was Irish, which it was (or is); this
  is how
His father says it, just as, being from Belfast, he calls the
  sink a 'jawbox'.

At first you think the screen's gone blank, till you realise the
  camera
Has focussed on the sink itself: it has eaten up the whole
Picture. Then it backtracks, to reveal a 'forties kitchen with
  a kind of wartime
Atmosphere: an old bakelite Clydesdale radio glows in the
  corner, humming
Over names like Moscow, Hilversum, Berlin. There's those
  jugs with blue and white
Striped bars, which give a premonition of the future (still
  our past) — filled
With flowers, they're *déjà vu* before their time, just as the
  sink, retired now
To the garden, overflows with hyacinths, geraniums.

There's something threatening about the kitchen — knives,
  glass, the epileptic

Buzzing of the overhead fluorescent strip, the white glaze
  blotched with calligraphic
Tea-leaves. Something in the pattern brings to mind an
  ornamental
Slightly murderous detail, and the picture changes with a
  click to show
The handcuffed metal *X*s of an old-style elevator gate.
  Someone's going down —
Chinese shadows flicking off and on across the various
  floors — to the Forensic Lab.
It's like suspicion, this weightless feeling in his stomach; and
  the clickety-clack
Reminds him of a railway journey, interrupted, for the
  seventh time that week,
By a bomb on the line between Dundalk and Newry. Or
  Newry and Dundalk, depending
Where you're coming from: like the difference between
  Cambodia and Kampuchea.

Shepherded on board an *Ulsterbus*, knowing now that the
  appointment won't be kept,
His attention wanders out across the rushy unkempt landscape, where a white dot
Concentrates his gaze. He lurches nearer. A hedge, a stone
  wall, gets in the way,
And then, brimming with water, wind-skimmed, rippled —
  he remembers how
He used to scoop an icy draught from it — the Belfast sink
  reveals itself.
It's now a cattle-trough, ripped out from a deconstructed
  farmhouse renovated
In the 'hacienda' style — not inappropriately, since *South of
  the Border*
Down Mexico Way is a big hit in these parts. Just then the
  border passes through him

Like a knife, invisibly, as the blip of the bus is captured on
   surveillance radar.

What's been stirring in his memory, like tea-leaves stirred in
   water —
He's elbow-deep in it, fingers trying to unblock the plug-
   hole — is the half-gnawed
Apple found at the *mise-en-scène*. The body, face-down on
   the steaming
Freshly-tarmacked road. He bites into the core, imagining
   his mouth's interior.
That twinge, an old occlusion. The tooth he broke on the rim
   of the jawbox
When he was eight. Blood-spattered white glaze; dilating, red
   confetti.
He spits out the pips and stares at the imaginary pith, seeing
   himself engraved there:
Furrows, indentations, grooves, as crisp as fingerprints. A
   little hinge of skin.

The mouth suggests the body —
Biting, grinding, breathing, chewing, spitting, tasting;
   clenched
In a grimace or a smile — his child's body, hunched in the
   dark alcove underneath
The sink, sulking, tearful, wishing he was dead. Imprisoned
   by so many
Small transgressions, he wants to break out of the trap. He's
   caught between
Bel*fast* and *Bel*fast, in the accordion pleats between two
   lurching carriages
Banging, rattling, threatening to break loose, as he gets a
   terrifying glimpse
Of railway sleepers, blotchy gravel flicking past a smell of
   creosote and oil and urine.

The coupling snaps; another mouth floats into view, its rust-
  tinged canine edges
Sealed in labelled see-through polythene; there's an O of
  condensation. From the cloud
A face begins to dawn: something like his own, but thicker,
  coarser, Jekyll
Turning into Hyde — an Englishman into an Irishman —
  emerging from the bloom
Behind the mirror. Breathed-on, becoming whole, the
  murderer is hunched
Behind the hedge. One bite from the apple, as the victim's
  Ford Fiesta trickles
Up the driveway. The car door opens. The apple's thrown
  away.

There's a breath of fresh tar. The scent will always summon
  up that afternoon,
As it blossoms into apple, into mouth. It's hanging in the air
  as Dr Jekyll finally
Makes it into Belfast. Beyond the steamed-up window, the
  half-dismantled gasworks
Loom up, like a rusty *film noir* laboratory — carboys, vats,
  alembics, coils, retorts.
It's that effect where one image warps into the other, like the
  double helix
Of the DNA code, his footsteps dogged throughout the action
  by another. Or
A split screen might suggest the parallels of past and present,
  Jekyll ticking
Downwards in the lift, as Hyde runs down the spiral stairwell.
  Till they meet.

What looks to us like a crackly newsreel, the picture jumping
  with flak,

Is the spotted, rust-tinged mirror screwed above the Belfast
  sink. Jekyll's head
Is jerking back and forward on the rim. Red confetti spatters
  the white glaze.
The camera backtracks to take in a tattered *Homes and*
  Gardens kitchen supplement.
A pair of hands — *lean, corded, knuckly, of a dusky pallor,*
  and thickly shadowed
With swart hair — come into view, and flick the pages of the
  magazine.
Bel*fast*, the voice says, not *Bel*fast. Then the credits roll.

John Ruskin in Belfast

As I approached the city, the storm-cloud of the Nineteenth
    Century
Began to wheel and mass its pendulous decades; the years
    grew weighty, slate-grey,
Palpable, muttering with dark caesurae, rolling in a clattering
    mockery
Of railway-luggage trains. All this while, the minutes seethed
    forth as artillery-smoke
Threatening to collapse into a dank fog. A single gauzy patch
    of iris blue —
All that remained of the free azure — contracted, shrank into
    oblivion
Till it became all pupil, olive-black, impenetrable; jagged
    migraine lightning
Flashed in the dark crock of my brain.

Like Turner, lashed to the mast of the *Ariel*, the better to see
    what he later painted —
The unwearied rage of memory, no distinction left between
    the sea and air —
I am riding out the hurricane, the writhing cloudscape of the
    sea collapsing
Into masses of accumulated yeast, which hang in ropes and
    wreaths from wave to wave;
Gouts and cataracts of foam pour from the smoky masts of
    the industrial Armada
As the wrack resolves itself in skeins and hanks, in terraces
    and sinks and troughs;
The air is sick with vitriol, the hospital-sweet scent of snuff,
    tobacco, linen.

And the labyrinthine alleyways are bloody with discarded
    bandages, every kind of ordure:

The dung of horses, dogs and rats and men; the knitted,
    knotted streets
Are crammed with old shoes, ashes, rags, smashed crockery,
    bullet casings, shreds
Of nameless clothes, rotten timber jaggy with bent nails,
    cinders, bones and half-bricks,
Broken bottles; and kneaded into, trampled, or heaving,
    fluttering, dancing
Over all of these, the tattered remnants of the news, every
    kind of foul advertisement,
The banner headlines that proclaim an oceanic riot, mutilated
    politics,
The seething yeast of anarchy: the very image of a pit, where
    a chained dwarf
Savages a chained bulldog.

As I strove against this lethargy and trance within myself,
    dismembered
Fragments of my speech, *The Mystery of Life and Its Arts*,
    swam up through the cumulus:
*This strange agony of desire for justice is often, I think, seen
    in Ireland —*
*For being generous-hearted, and intending always to do right,
    you still neglect*
*External laws of right, and therefore you do wrong, without
    conceiving of it;*
*And so fly into wrath when thwarted, and will not admit the
    possibility of error . . . .*
*See how in the static mode of ancient Irish art, the missal-painter
    draws his angel*
*With no sense of failure, as a child might draw an angel, putting
    red dots*
*In the palm of each hand, while the eyes — the eyes are perfect
    circles, and,*
I regret to say, the mouth is left out altogether.

That blank mouth, like the memory of a disappointed smile,
 comes back to haunt me.
That calm terror, closed against the smog and murk of Belfast:
 Let it not open
That it might condemn me. Let it remain inviolate.
Or let that missing mouth be mine, as, one evening in Siena
I walked the hills above, where fireflies moved like finely-
 broken starlight
Through the purple leaves, rising, falling, as the cobalt
 clouds — white-edged, mountainous —
Surged into thunderous night; and fireflies gusted everywhere,
 mixed with the lightning,
Till I thought I'd open up my mouth and swallow them, as I
 might gulp the Milky Way.

When the last star fades into the absolute azure, I will return
To where *The Dawn of Christianity*, by Turner, hangs in
 Belfast in its gilt frame:
Airy, half-discovered shades of aqua, the night becoming hazy
 milk and pearl,
The canvas is a perfect circle; and as I gaze into its opalescent
 mirror
I try to find its subject, *The Flight into Egypt*. A palm tree
 beckons
Like an angel's hand: words issue from the sealed tomb of
 his mouth — *Be thou there*
Until I bring thee word — and the Holy Family vanishes into
 the breathed-on mirror
Where the Nile-blue sky becomes the Nile, abandoning the
 Empire
To its Massacre of Innocents, the mutilated hands and knees
 of children.

Narrative in Black and White

Now take these golf balls, scattered all around the place,
which since
The reproduction's blurred, you'd easily misconstrue as
ping-pong —
You can't make out the dimples. But they're different as
chalk and cheese:
Ever get hit by a golf ball? You'd know all about it. And
perhaps
The golf club in the bottom corner is no give-away. People
have been known
To mistake it for a gun. And the disembodied plus-fours
Might be army surplus. No, all these things are dangerous
enough,
According to whose rules you play. Which is maybe why
they're put there,
Where you'd least expect them, floating against the
façade of the Europa.

Hotel, that is. You know it? Looks as if it's taken from a
photograph,
Down to the missing *E* of the logo, the broken windows,
which they only got
Around to fixing last week. Things drift off like that, or
people drift in.
Like Treacy, who it's all about, according to the guy who
painted it.
This splash of red here: not blood, but a port-wine stain or
strawberry mark
That Treacy carried all his life, just here, above the wrist-
watch. Any time
You saw him sitting, he would have his right hand over it.
Like this.
Too easily recognised, he didn't like. This is where the black
gloves

Come in, gripping the revolving foyer doors. Or maybe one
  of them
Is raised, like saying *Power* — to the people, to himself,
  whatever.

Billiard balls? Well, maybe. Certainly these random scratches
  on the canvas
Suggest the chalk-marks on a green baize, a faded diagram
  from which
You'd try to piece together what the action was. Like trying
  to account
For Treacy's movements. Though on the night in question,
  according to the barman
In The Beaten Docket, he'd staggered in from some win on
  the horses,
Slaps a tenner on the counter, and orders a 'Blue Angel'.
  Blue what?
Says the barman. Angel, Treacy says, Blue Bols, vodka, ice,
  a drop of sugar.
Oh, and top it up with whipped cream. I say this just to show
  the sort
Of him, like someone who a year or two ago would not have
  known 'cocktail'
From a hen's arse. You're sure, the barman says, you
  wouldn't like a straw?

The staircase is important. The zig-zag is like taking one
  step forward,
Two steps back. For who would take the stairs up thirteen
  floors, when
He could take the lift? The reason why, the power had gone
  that night.
So only one way in, and one way out. As sure as meeting
  your own shadow.

This, I think, is what the mirror represents. Like, everybody
knew about the split,
And what side Treacy ended up on. Of course, the detail's
lost;
You have to see it like it is, original. The colours, the
dimensions.
Even the frame, like someone spying through binoculars, is
saying something:
I'm watching you; but you, you can't see me. Ping-pong.
Yin-yang.

So here is Treacy, at the wrong end of the telescope,
diminishing.
He was seen in this bar, that bar. Like what I'm saying is,
that anybody
Might have fingered him. So the man on the thirteenth floor
sits pat.
He draws back the curtain. He stares through the kaleidoscope
of snow
And sees what's coming next. Treacy's footsteps. Game, set
and match.
They found him in the empty room. The face was blown
off. They rolled down
One black glove. A Rorschach blot. The Red Hand, as he
called himself.
Me? I knew him like a brother. Once. But then our lives
grew parallel, if
Parallel is never meeting. He started dressing up and talking
down. What
He would and wouldn't do. And people don't go shooting
off their mouths like that.

Hamlet

As usual, the clock in The Clock Bar was a good few minutes
fast:
A fiction no one really bothered to maintain, unlike the
story
The comrade on my left was telling, which no one knew for
certain truth:
*Back in 1922, a sergeant, I forget his name, was shot outside
the National Bank* . . . .
Ah yes, what year was it that they knocked it down? Yet, its
memory's as fresh
As the inky smell of new pound notes — which interferes
with the beer-and-whiskey
Tang of now, like two dogs meeting in the revolutionary 69
of a long sniff,
Or cattle jostling shit-stained flanks in the Pound. For *pound*,
as some wag
Interrupted, was an off-shoot of the Falls, from the Irish,
fál, a hedge;
Hence, *any kind of enclosed thing*, its twigs and branches
commemorated
By the soldiers' drab and olive camouflage, as they try to
melt
Into a brick wall; red coats might be better, after all. *At any
rate,
This sergeant's number came up; not a winning one. The
bullet had his name on it.*
Though Sergeant X, as we'll call him, doesn't really feature
in the story:
The nub of it is, *This tin can which was heard that night,
trundling down
From the bank, down Balaclava Street. Which thousands
heard, and no one ever
Saw. Which was heard for years, any night that trouble might
be*

Round the corner . . . and when it skittered to a halt, you knew
That someone else had snuffed it: a name drifting like an afterthought,
A scribbled wisp of smoke you try and grasp, as it becomes diminuendo, then
Vanishes. For *fál* is also *frontier, boundary*, as in *the undiscovered country*
From whose bourne no traveller returns, the illegible, thorny hedge of time itself —
Heartstopping moments, measured not by the pulse of a wrist-watch, nor
The archaic anarchists' alarm-clock, but a mercury tilt device
Which 'only connects' on any given bump on the road. So, by this wingèd messenger
The promise 'to pay the bearer' is fulfilled:

As someone buys another round, an Allied Irish Banks £10 note drowns in
The slops of the counter; a Guinness stain blooms on the artist's impression
Of the sinking of *The Girona*; a tiny foam hisses round the salamander brooch
Dredged up to show how love and money endure, beyond death and the Armada,
Like the bomb-disposal expert in his suit of salamander-cloth.
Shielded against the blast of time by a strangely-mediaeval visor,
He's been outmoded by this jerky robot whose various attachments include
A large hook for turning over corpses that may be booby-trapped;

But I still have this picture of his hands held up to avert the
    future
In a final act of *No surrender*, as, twisting through the murky
    fathoms
Of what might have been, he is washed ashore as pearl and
    coral.

This strange *eruption to our state* is seen in other versions of
    the Falls:
A no-go area, a ghetto, a demolition zone. For the ghost, as
    it turns out —
All this according to your man, and I can well believe it —
    this tin ghost,
Since the streets it haunted were abolished, was never heard
    again.
The sleeve of Raglan Street has been unravelled; the helmet
    of Balaclava
Is torn away from the mouth. The dim glow of Garnet has
    gone out,
And with it, all but the memory of where I lived. I, too, heard
    the ghost:
A roulette trickle, or the hesitant annunciation of a downpour,
    ricochetting
Off the window; a goods train shunting distantly into a siding,
Then groaning to a halt; the rainy cries of children after dusk.
For the voice from the grave reverberates in others' mouths,
    as the sails
Of the whitethorn hedge swell up in a little breeze, and tremble
Like the spiral blossom of Andromeda: so suddenly are
    shrouds and branches
Hung with street-lights, celebrating all that's lost, as fields
    are reclaimed
By the Starry Plough. So we name the constellations, to put
    a shape

On what was there; so, the storyteller picks his way between
the isolated stars.

But, *Was it really like that?* And, *Is the story true?*
You might as well tear off the iron mask, and find that no one,
after all,
Is there: nothing but a cry, a summons, clanking out from
the smoke
Of demolition. Like some son looking for his father, or the
father for his son,
We try to piece together the exploded fragments. Let these
broken spars
Stand for the Armada and its proud full sails, for even if
The clock is put to rights, everyone will still believe it's fast:
The barman's shouts of *time* will be ignored in any case,
since time
Is conversation; it is the hedge that flits incessantly into the
present,
As words blossom from the drinkers' mouths, and the flotilla
returns to harbour,
Long after hours.

Second Language

English not being yet a language, I wrapped my lubber-lips
    around my thumb;
Brain-deaf as an embryo, I was snuggled in my comfort-
    blanket dumb.

Growling figures campaniled above me, and twanged their
    carillons of bronze
Sienna consonants embedded with the vowels *alexandrite,*
    emerald and *topaz.*

The topos of their discourse seemed to do with me and
    convoluted genealogy;
Wordy whorls and braids and skeins and spiral helices,
    unskeletoned from laminate geology —

How this one's slate-blue gaze is correspondent to
    another's new-born eyes;
Gentians, forget-me-nots, and cornflowers, diurnal in a
    heliotrope surmise.

Alexandrine tropes came gowling out like beagles, loped and
    unroped
On a snuffly Autumn. Nimrod followed after with his bold
    Arapahoes,

Who whooped and hollered in their unforked tongue. The
    trail was starred with
Myrrh and frankincense of Anno Domini; the Wise Men
    wisely paid their tariff.

A single star blazed at my window. Crepuscular, its acoustic
    perfume dims
And swells like flowers on the stanzaic-papered wall.
    Shipyard hymns

Then echoed from the East: gantry-clank and rivet-ranks,
    Six-County hexametric
Brackets, bulkheads, girders, beams, and stanchions;
    convocated and Titanic.

Leviathans of rope snarled out from ropeworks: disgorged
    hawsers, unkinkable lay,
Ratlines, S-twists, plaited halyards, Z-twists, catlines; all had
    their say.

Tobacco-scent and snuff breathed out in gouts of factory
    smoke like aromatic camomile;
Sheaves of brick-built mill-stacks glowered in the sulphur-
    mustard fog like campaniles.

The dim bronze noise of midnight-noon and Angelus then
    boomed and clinked in Latin
Conjugations; statues wore their shrouds of amaranth; the
    thurible chinked out its smoky patina.

I inhaled *amo, amas, amat* in quids of *pros* and *versus* and
    Introibos
Ad altare Dei; incomprehensibly to others, spoke in Irish. I
    slept through the Introit.

The enormous Monastery surrounded me with nave and
    architrave. Its ornate pulpit
Spoke to me in fleurs-de-lys of Purgatory. Its sacerdotal
    gaze became my pupil.

My pupil's nose was bathed in Pharaonic unguents of dope
    and glue.
Flimsy tissue-paper plans of aeroplanes unfolded whimsical
    ideas of the blue,

Where, unwound, the prop's elastic is unpropped and balsa-
    wood extends its wings
Into the hazardous azure of April. It whirrs into the realm
    of things.

Things are kinks that came in tubes; like glue or paint
    extruded, that became
A hieroglyphic alphabet. Incestuous in pyramids, Egyptians
    were becalmed.

I climbed into it, delved its passageways, its sepulchral
    interior, its things of kings
Embalmed; sarcophagi, whose perfume I exhumed in chancy
    versions of the *I-Ching*.

A chink of dawn was revelated by the window. Far-off cocks
    crowed crowingly
And I woke up, verbed and tensed with speaking English; I
    lisped the words so knowingly.

I love the as-yet morning, when no one's abroad, and I am
    like a postman on his walk,
Distributing strange messages and bills, and arbitrations with
    the world of talk:

I foot the snow and almost-dark. My shoes are crisp, and
    bite into the blue-
White firmament of pavement. My father holds my hand and
    goes blah-

Blah with me into the ceremonial dawn. I'm wearing tweed.
    The universe is Lent
And Easter is an unspun cerement, the gritty, knitty, tickly
    cloth of unspent

Time. I feel its warp and weft. Bobbins pirn and shuttle in
    Imperial
Typewriterspeak. I hit the keys. The ribbon-black clunks
    out the words in serial.

What comes next is next, and no one knows the *che sarà* of
    it, but must allow
The *Tipp-Ex* present at the fingertips. Listen now: an angel
    whispers of the here-and-now.

The future looms into the mouth incessantly, gulped-at and
    unspoken;
Its guardian is intangible, but gives you hints and winks and
    nudges as its broken token.

I woke up blabbering and dumb with too much sleep. I rubbed
    my eyes and ears.
I closed my eyes again and flittingly, forgetfully, I glimpsed
    the noise of years.

Eesti

I wandered homesick-lonely through that Saturday of silent
    Tallinn
When a carillon impinged a thousand raining quavers on my
    ear, tumbling

Dimly from immeasurable heights into imaginary brazen
    gong-space, trembling
Dimpled in their puddled, rain-drop halo-pools, concentric-
    ally assembling.

I glimpsed the far-off, weeping onion-domes. I was inveigled
    towards the church
Through an aural labyrinth of streets until I sheltered in its
    porch.

I thumbed the warm brass worn thumb-scoop of the latch.
    Tock. I entered into bronze-
Dark, shrines and niches lit by beeswax tapers and the sheen
    of ikons.

Their eyes and the holes in their hands were nailed into my
    gaze, *quod erat demonstrandum*:
Digits poised and pointed towards their hearts. They are
    beautiful Panjandrums

Invoked by murmuring and incense, hymns that father passes
    on to father,
The patina of faces under painted faces. They evoke another

Time, where I am going with you, father, to first Mass. We
    walked
The starry frozen pavement, holding hands to stop ourselves
    from falling. There was no talk,

Nor need for it. Our incense-breath was words enough as
　　we approached the Gothic,
Shivering in top-coats, on the verge of sliding off the metro-
　　nomic

Azure-gradual dawn, as nave and transept summoned us
　　with beaded, thumbed
And fingered whispering. Silk-tasselled missals. Rosaries.
　　Statues stricken dumb

Beneath their rustling purple shrouds, as candles wavered in
　　the holy smoke.
The mosaic chapel echoed with a clinking, chinking censer-
　　music.

This red-letter day would not be written, had I not wandered
　　through the land of Eesti.
I asked my father how he thought it went. He said to me in
　　Irish, *Listen: Éist*.

Apparat

Unparalysed, the robot bomb-disposal expert inched and
   tacked across the mezzanine
As casually as someone to be barbered sits relaxing with a
   magazine.

It was using 'deep creep' and 'infinite hair', conversing in its
   base-of-two conundrum.
Its chips were bugged like all the toasters in the apparatchniks'
   condominium.

Turnbull twiddled with the radio controls. He twitched his
   robot's claws.
He felt the Mobile Ordinance Disposal Unit index through
   its dictionary of clues.

Umbilical, he was in the waiting room. Barberlike, he opened
   up his case of instruments.
He was beckoned by the realms of Nod. He entered in with
   incense and Byzantine vestments.

The smart bomb got the message and intoned the right
   liturgical analysis.
Latinate, they swapped explosive bits and pieces; they re-
   emerged in Nemesis.

The Brain of Edward Carson

They cracked the skull and watched its two halves creak
apart, like the decks
Of some Byzantine trireme. The herringboned, zipped oars,
the chains and shackles.
The bronze circuitry. The locks. The Titanic, legal depositions
of the cells.
The hammered rivets. The rivetted, internal gaze. The screws.
The nails.
The caulked bulwarks. The slaves, embalmed in honeycomb
prismatic.

Barbaric instruments inserted there, like hook and razor,
iron picks
By which they will extrapolate its history: the bronze, eternal
static
Of his right, uplifted hand. The left hand like a shield. The
bolted-on, external
Eyes. The seraphic frown. The borders and the chains
contained therein. The fraternal
Gaze of the Exclusive Brethren: orange and bruised purple,
cataleptic.

The map of Ulster opened up, hexagonal and intricate,
tectonic:
Its shifting plates were clunked and welded into place by
laws Masonic.
The ladder and the rope. The codicils. The compasses by
which they sail
Uncharted futures. The outstretched hand. The crown. The
sash. The secret nail.
And then disintegration intervened, the brain eluded them:
Sphinxlike, catatonic.

Opus 14

Hole Blown in Baroque Splendour of Opera House (designed
  by Frank Matcham):
The Security Forces were specifically looking for terrorists
  but spectacularly failed to catch them.

❧

Newly-appointed innumerate Chancellor of the Exchequer
  What-Do-You-Call-Him Clarke
Was counting his stars in twos like the innumerable animals
  in Noah's Ark.

❧

Did you know that 'the set of all objects describable in
  exactly eleven English words'
Is called an 'R-Set'? I didn't. It was dreamed up by the
  people who put the 'surd' in 'absurd'.

❧

Spokesman for censored political party spoke in someone
  else's lip-synch
So perfectly, you'd think it was the man himself, though
  much of this is double-think.

❧

So I woke up this morning with yet another wrong solution
  to Fermat's Last
Theorem, which bore about the same relationship to global
  X as does the world to Atlas.

❧

He had a pocketful of pocket calculators, palindromes, and
    anagrams. The Name
Of Names eluded him as yet, but he was working on it and
    had found the Name of the Game.

~

The idea was that one and one made three, like in the Holy
    Family
Or Trinity, where 'three' is pronounced 'tree', as in the Irish
    Christian Brother's homily.

~

I think this goes to show that Cajori's study of mathematical
    symbols
Is in part, like not to see the wood for trees, a graveyard for
    dead symbols.

~

For you can deconstruct all sorts of words from 'England':
    angel, *gland* and *dangle*;
It's the way the Germans have captured the Gaolainn-speaking
    industry in Dingle.

~

Sums are funny. *Wars 2. Legs 1. Wives 2. Children 4. Wounds
    2. Total 11.* You know?
Which reminds me to go and check out Nik Cohn's book *Yes,
    We Have No.*

~

Bananas is understood. It's not known by many, or maybe it
   is, that Cohn's from Londonderry or Derry,
Which might account for the ambivalence of the fact of the
   Foyle's not having a ferry.

◆

Of course, it has this double-decker bridge, at which you're
   doubly checked.
The soldier looks at you and then he looks at your picture.
   It's pronounced *echt*.

◆

At the previous Chancellor's Last Supper, he was seized by a
   sudden triskaidecaphobia
Which took him to the fourteenth floor, where he became
   immersed in a conference of bankers from the Bank of
   Wachovia.

◆

It likes to do that. *Wachovia*. Which brings me back to
   baroque Opera House designed by Frank.
The googolplex security net had been full of innumerable
   holes held together by string, to be frank.

All Souls

The un*Walkman* headphones stick out awkwardly, because
 they are receiving
Not the packaged record of a song, but real-time input, a form
 of blah
Alive with intimations of mortality, the loud and unclear
 garbled static.

It's the peripatetic buzz of static, like it was a Hallowe'en-like
 weather
That you rarely get at Hallowe'en. The mushrooms mushroomed
 as per
Usual, that is to say, in subterfuge, slowly dawning through
 on Instamatic.

Like putting on spectacles, when what it was was blurred,
 then swims
Into your focus. You can see they come from the Planet X,
 with their walkie-
Talkies, the heavy warbling of their heavy Heaney tyres and
 automatic,

Gyroscope-type-tank-surveillance technique, their faces
 blacked like
Boots. Their antennae quivered on that Hallowe'en
 encountered just beyond Sans
Souci. It was, in fact, outside the Fire Station, and the firemen, with Platonic

Abandon, were going through their exercises, rehearsing for
 the Fire,
The Bomb, the Incident, some routine dot on the dial, where
 the wireless
Lights with intimations of Hilversum or Moscow, and the
 Radio Symphonic

Orchestra is playing someone's Dead March through the
  whistles and the static
Of the dark you listen to. To which you listen, like routine
  intimations
Of the precinct where the oblique Mandarins decreed
  antique

Examinations. Then the sound was turned up suddenly,
  anorectic candidates
Blew their fuses; they had failed to comprehend their
  hierophantic elders, who
Laid the rubric down so many yonks ago in ancient mnemonic.

Demonic intimations went on daily; routine, undercover
  orchestrations
Of the nominated discipline of alphabetic, proscribed areas
That ended, as they always do, in tragic, tired recriminations;
  rhetoric.

It then occurred the Firemen had a Ball, it was at Hallowe'en.
  Ecstatically, they
Didn't have false faces on. They were plastic, not explosively,
  but faces. Then
They tore their faces off. Un*Walkman*like. Laconic.
  Workmanlike.

58

They'd rehearsed the usual Heinz variety of condoms, clocks,
    fertilizer, and electrical flex,
Plus a Joker's device which, someone claimed, had devolved
    from one of the '50s *Batman* serial flicks —
Which proves there's nothing new *sub specie aeternitatis*, or
    it's part of the general, Heraclitean flux.

Like the orange-sized plastic tomato that glows on the Formica
    counter of the all-night caff,
Your actual's slantindicular as the letter zed, and a long shot
    from being all kiff,
As you'd guess from the blobs and squiggles they'd squidged
    on their chips and someone got on his cuff.

It was raining on the neon writing as they upped and offed
    and packed themselves into the pick-up truck;
The drizzly sound of the words seeped out and will-o'-the-
    wisped on the nearby railway track;
But when the deal came down and the *Enterprise* glimmed
    through, they'd be *n* cards short of a trick.

For they couldn't computate how many beans made five; a
    has-been Celticamerad had vizzed them to the Picts.
And, chauffed through the dark, they were well on the drag
    to becoming commemorative plaques —
Which is hickery-pickery, Indian smoke to the pipe of the
    aberkayheybo Hibernian Pax.

So it's mercury tilt and quicksilver flash as the Johnson
    slammed on the brakes
And it's indecipherababble bits and bods, skuddicked and
    scrabbled like alphabet bricks —
A red hand. A rubber glove. The skewed grin of the clock.
A clip of ammunition. A breastpocketful of *Bics*.

Opus Operandi

1

Fatima handed out twelve teaching modules of the 'empathy
  belly'
To the variously expectant fathers. Some were Paddy, and
  some were Billy.

Today's lesson was the concept 'Orange'. They parsed it into
  segments: some were kith,
And some were kin. They spat out the pips and learned to
  peel the pith.

Then the deep grammar of the handshake, the shibboleths of
  aitch and *haitch*:
It's a bit like tying knots, whether Gordian or sheepshank,
  clove or hitch.

In the half-dark of their lapidary parliament, you can just
  make out the shape
Of chimeras and minotaurs. Anthropomorphic goats are
  blethering to the demi-sheep.

It seems the gene-pool got contaminated. Everything was
  neither one thing nor the other;
So now they're trying to agree on a formula for a petition to
  the Author.

He's working overtime just now, dismembering a goose for
  goose-quills.
Tomorrow will be calfskin parchment, then the limitation
  clauses and the codicils.

2

Jerome imagined Babel with its laminates and overlapping
  tongues
And grooves, the secret theatre with its clamps and vices,
  pincers, tongs.

It's like an Ark or quinquereme he prised apart, to find the
  little oarsmen
At their benches. They looked somewhat surprised as he began
  the seminar

On hieroglyphs, using them as prime examples. They began to
  strain
Against the shackles of his language, his sentences, his full-
  stop and his chain.

He tapped the clinker-built antique and it disgorged its
  clichés.
He upturned it and it struggled like a turtle full of cogs and
  helices.

A school of clocks swarmed out from the Underwood's
  overturned undercarriage,
Full of alphabetical intentions, led astray by braggadocio
  and verbiage.

Typecast letters seethed on the carpet, trying to adopt its
  garbled Turkish
Convolutions. They were baffled by the script's *auctoritas*.

Bug-like, they attached themselves to the underside of the
  rug and hung there
Bat-like, colonised in non-pareils and minions, hugger-
  mugger.

3

Dr Moreau contemplated the Doormouse. It was wearing an
  elegant penguin
Suit. Moreau handed it his hat and went on in. He hoped the
  operetta would be sanguine.

Die Fledermaus was dressed up in his usual bat-suit.
  Crocodile-
Skin shoes. A cape for wings, and an absolutely Dracula-like

Dicky-bow. An as-yet-unbloodied bib. He bared his fangs
  as far back as the epiglottis
And began to aria an echolalia of aspirates and glottal stops.

Eventually he found a disguised Countess, and sunk an umlaut
  in her jugular.
He gargled in her tautonyms and phonemes, her Transyl-
  vanian corpuscular.

Her eyes drooled and grew as he imbibed her, as they glided
  through the mirror
And came out on the other side; then, clinging to each other,
  dimmed into tomorrow.

Moreau's yesterday was their tomorrow. His fossil study of
  the pterodactyl
Had led him to believe that man could fly, fuelled by iambics,
  alcohol, and dactyls.

Jerome drank the vision in. He put on his airman's snorkel
  and got into the bubble.
He gave the thumbs-up sign, and set the ultrasonic scan for
  Babel.

In his amphibian, the hero limped home in a grand Byronic Gesture; Fatima dismissed the Twelve; it was the end of therapy and embryonics.

The Ballad of HMS Belfast

On the first of April, *Belfast* disengaged her moorings, and
    sailed away
From old Belfast. Sealed orders held our destination, some-
    where in the Briny Say.

Our crew of Jacks was aromatic with tobacco-twist and
    alcoholic
Reekings from the night before. Both Catestants and
    Protholics,

We were tarry-breeked and pig-tailed, and sailed beneath the
    White Ensign;
We loved each other nautically, though most landlubbers
    thought we were insane.

We were full-rigged like the *Beagle*, piston-driven like the
    Enterprise
Express; each system was a back-up for the other, auxiliar-
    izing verse with prose.

Our engines ticked and tacked us up the Lough, cranks and
    link-pins, cross-rods
Working ninety to the dozen; our shrouds and ratlines rattled
    like a cross-roads

Dance, while swivels, hook blocks, cleats, and fiddles jigged
    their semi-colons
On the staves. We staggered up the rigging like a bunch of
    demi-golems,

Tipsy still, and dreamed of underdecks — state-rooms, crystal
    chandeliers,
And saloon bars — until we got to gulp the ozone; then we
    swayed like gondoliers

Above the aqua. We gazed at imperceptible horizons, where
    amethyst
Dims into blue, and pondered them again that night, before
    the mast.

Some sang of Zanzibar and Montalban, and others of the lands
    unascertained
On maps; we entertained the Phoenix and the Unicorn, till
    we were grogged and concertina'ed.

We've been immersed, since then, in cruises to the Podes and
    Antipodes;
The dolphin and the flying fish would chaperone us like
    aquatic aunties

In their second, mermaid childhood, till we ourselves felt
    neither fish nor flesh, but
Breathed through gills of rum and brandy. We'd flounder on
    the randy decks like halibut.

Then our Captain would emerge to scold us from his three
    days' incommunicado
And promenaded on the poop-deck, sashed and epauletted
    like a grand Mikado

To bribe us with the Future: new Empires, Realms of Gold,
    and precious ore
Unheard-of since the days of Homer: we'd boldly go where
    none had gone before.

Ice to Archangel, tea to China, coals to Tyne: such would be
    our cargo.
We'd confound the speculators' markets and their exchequered,
    logical embargo.

Then were we like the *Nautilus*, that trawls the vast and
  purple catacomb
For cloudy shipwrecks, settled in their off-the-beam,
  intractable aplomb.

Electric denizens glide through the Pisan masts, flickering
  their Pisces' *lumière*;
We regard them with a Cyclops eye, from our bathyscope
  beneath *la mer*.

Scattered cutlery and dinner-services lie, hugger-mugger, on
  the murky floor.
An empty deck-chair yawns and undulates its awning like a
  semaphore.

Our rising bubble then went *bloop*, *bloop* till it burst the
  swaying window-pane;
Unfathomed from the cobalt deep, we breathed the broad
  Pacific once again.

Kon-Tiki-like, we'd drift for days, abandoning ourselves to
  all the elements,
Guided only by the aromatic coconut, till the wind brought
  us the scent of lemons —

Then we'd disembark at Vallambroso or Gibraltar to explore
  the bars;
Adorned in sequin-scales, we glimmered phosphorescently
  like stars

That crowd innumerably in midnight harbours. O olive-
  dark interior,
All splashed with salt and wine! Havana gloom within the
  humidor!

The atmosphere dripped heavy with the oil of anchovies,
  tobacco-smoke, and chaw;
We grew languorous with grass and opium and *kif*, the very
  best of draw,

And sprawled in urinous piazzas; slept until the fog-horn
  trump of Gabriel.
We woke, and rubbed our eyes, half-gargled still with
  braggadocio and garble.

And then the smell of docks and ropeworks. Horse-dung.
  The tolling of the Albert clock.
Its Pisan slant. The whirring of its ratchets. Then everything
  began to click:

I lay bound in iron chains, alone, my *aisling* gone, my sentence
  passed.
Grey Belfast dawn illuminated me, on board the prison ship
  Belfast.

Note

All of these poems appear in books published by The Gallery Press: 'Dunne' in *The New Estate and Other Poems* (1988); the poems on pages 13–52 in *The Irish for No* (1987); and those on pages 53–94 in *Belfast Confetti* (1989). 'Second Language' and the poems on pages 101–116 were collected in *First Language* (1993); and 'Eesti' in *Opera Et Cetera* (1996).

Bloodaxe Books published editions of *The Irish for No*, *Belfast Confetti* and *Opera Et Cetera*.